MY NATURE
MY WORLD

DR. RAJESH CHAUHAN

BLUEROSE PUBLISHERS
India | U.K.

Copyright © Dr. Rajesh Chauhan 2024

All rights reserved by author. No part of this publication may be reproduced, stored in a retrieval system or transmitted in any form or by any means, electronic, mechanical, photocopying, recording or otherwise, without the prior permission of the author. Although every precaution has been taken to verify the accuracy of the information contained herein, the publisher assumes no responsibility for any errors or omissions. No liability is assumed for damages that may result from the use of information contained within.

BlueRose Publishers takes no responsibility for any damages, losses, or liabilities that may arise from the use or misuse of the information, products, or services provided in this publication.

For permissions requests or inquiries regarding this publication, please contact:

BLUEROSE PUBLISHERS
www.BlueRoseONE.com
info@bluerosepublishers.com
+91 8882 898 898
+4407342408967

ISBN: 978-93-6452-855-9

Cover Image from AI
Cover design: Shivam
Typesetting: Namrata Saini

First Edition: 2021
Second Edition: August 2024

Lives so Blessed!

I dedicate this book in loving gratitude to my parents, (Late) Mrs. Krishna Kumari and Mr. Balwant Singh (Retired Commissioner of Income Tax), who have left on us an indelible mark while inculcating creative abilities amongst all family members up to the next generation. Life took a major change when my mother suddenly left us in her sleep, on the morning of 5 October 2020, to continue with her onward journey!

Contents

Preface 6
Acknowledgements 9
Foreword 11

1. Namaste 13
2. Of Power and Mind 15
3. Nature Gave Us, Did We? 16
4. My Nature, My World 21
5. The Time Is Changing 24
6. Manipulating Nature 26
7. Break of Dawn 29
8. Floods All Over 32
9. Every Dark Cloud has a Silver Lining 36
10. Nothing Stays the Same 40
11. World Times 41
12. The Midas Touch 44
13. The Man, the Keeper 47
14. Power of Logic 53
15. Naturally Yours Play Me 55
16. Himalayan Tsunami 57
17. Tolerance Eclipsed 60
18. The Cry of the Day 61
19. Blocked and Choked 63

20. Population over a Billion 64
21. Death a Life Anew 66
22. Once in a Life Time.. 69

Preface

I hail from medical profession and have been working as an anesthesiologist, switching over from general anesthesia to working exclusively in the highly specialized field of Cardiac Anesthesia and Intensive Care, very early on in my career, as early as January 1989.

I have always been interested in the environment and have contributed towards plantation of 200 trees (all that I could) in a mega project called "Cauvery Calling Initiative" an independent movement by the spiritual leader Sadhguru in the Cauvery basin area, where there is a huge risk of desertification in the times to come. Already over 55 million trees have been planted in the last few years and the process is continuing, a welcome step to resolve crisis laden ecological imbalances, a by-product of scientific research in the last 200 years.

After graduating from Mahatma Gandhi Institute of Medical Sciences, Sevagram, I chose Anesthesiology as my field of specialization and obtained a postgraduate degree from the Government Medical College, Nagpur in 1985. I later joined Escorts Heart Institute and Research Centre, New Delhi in January 1989. I continued to work there for 25 years with eminent cardiac surgeons and cardiologists. Thereafter, I had short stints in other premier institutions in New Delhi.

The writing of poems came to me during blank moments, when I transformed my thoughts into productive scripts. The development was a slow process. I started writing on current topics appearing in the newspapers. My first piece was on the population explosion, when the country had hit one billion in 2000. My attention was then directed towards subjects like man-made excesses that have disturbed nature, threatening our ecology and with that, the very existence and survival of our earth, in fact the only "Blue Planet" known to exist in the Universe, is now a dying planet. The thought of finding a new "Earth" are being reported increasingly. Have we lost hope in saving our own planet? The planet, which has supported life for millions of years and now after creating problems we are planning to abandon it and migrate to an uninhabited one, many light years away from Earth. Whether the mission succeeds or not is another question but to make it a success has led to heightened emission of pollutants by the scientists busy developing rockets and launching them one after another. This has not been helpful in applying brakes on things that promote changes in nature. Instead, it has added to rising temperatures and sea levels across the World. There have been mistakes committed in managing many aspects affecting life all over the country and worldwide, which have been the cause of innumerable tragedies. The latest being the COVID-19 pandemic due to the disruptive one- upmanship prevailing amongst nations. People are facing a crisis of survival. The pandemic is causing the death of millions of people worldwide, while the basic issue of its starting point remains unresolved, till date.

I have tried to touch various topics in the form of poems in the following pages that the readers may find interesting.

Dr. Rajesh Chauhan
MD Anesthesia
20 July 2021

Acknowledgements

I take an opportunity to thank my parents, Mr. Balwant Singh and (Late) Mrs. Krishna Kumari who have always inspired me to do something to leave an indelible presence of my life. My mother who passed away in October 2020 has gone through many of these poems and her expressions after going through the scripts were enough to convey her feelings, which I will carry throughout my life. My wife, Dr. Vibha Chauhan has had an incredible influence on me and used to find it difficult while I used to keep hanging on my mobile writing scripts but later always helped me in bringing about changes that helped me modify the text.

My daughter, Vishakha Chauhan, is endowed with special writing skills has been joyfully critical in finding out mistakes, so also is true for Dr. Hima Chauhan, and my son Devansh Chauhan (no mean guiding force and a constant source that forces me to keep working); have been encouraging me with constructive criticism and helping me to edit manuscripts all along. Besides scores of friends, my former colleagues with whom I have worked for many years and batch mates from medical college have always persuaded me to continue in my area of interest, which has now culminated in the form of poems that are compiled in this book.

I also acknowledge the contribution of the publishing team from "BlueRose Publishers Pvt. Ltd.", for having given the final shape to this book titled, My Nature, My World, a collection of poems which I devote to all avid readers!

Dr. Rajesh Chauhan
MD Anesthesia

Foreword

As a reader with strong interest in both poetry and environment, I found the book "My Nature, My World", written by Dr. Rajesh Chauhan, captivating. This collection of poems is a sincere attempt of the author for preserving our planet. Dr. Chauhan, an anesthesiologist by profession, has used his observational skills to throw some light on the most important environmental issues of our time.

Each poem in this collection is a powerful message that speaks to the current state of our natural world. Titles such as "Time is Changing," "Population over Billion," and "Nature Gave Us, Did We?" resonate deeply, pointing out our collective responsibility towards Earth. The author's poetry reminds us of how life of our environment is short termed and that there is an urgent need to protect it.

Poem "Himalaya Tsunami," is a strong message that nature's destruction is the consequence of human negligence. The blessed river became a curse for the Himalayan Disaster.

In "The Man the Keeper," the author describes that humans are like guardians of nature. "World Times" and "Manipulating Nature" further explore the interrelationship between human actions and environmental changes.

The book "My Nature, My World" is a thought provoking work that gives the message of environmental accountability. The author's work inspires to become more active in environmental conservation. I look forward to read more works on this subject and hope that the author continues to share his insights on the same.

Sunil Singh
Dehradun
28 June 2024

1
Namaste

Namaste!
A welcome sign!
To parting away,
From I know it all,
To, I don't know anything.
Am I available?
To, don't consider me even!
Namaste says it all!
From being apologetic,
To, snubbing away,
Extended to stranger,
From morning till evening!
Used in the sub-continent,
In Covid times!
Spread all over,
Greeting from distance,
Used in sports events,
By Statesmen,
In all forums,
Sign of "Sanatan-Dharma"!

Accepted now all over,
A silent sign!
Expressions on face,
Action so gracious,
Hands folded for "Namaste"!
Says it all!

2
Of Power and Mind

An interesting fact of science,
Muscles for efficiency,
Fat for mind,
Muscles for monsters,
Powerless in mind!
For mind amongst monsters,
Small in size,
Physically weak,
May be strong in mind!
Fat forms most of the brain,
But efficiency is considered fine.
It is fat versus efficiency,
Proteins versus mind!
Who is the winner or loser?
Can't make up my mind!

3
Nature Gave Us, Did We?

The way it came to life,
Would go the same way!
Born with a Big-Bang,
Big-Crunch will take it away!

Billions of years to come to life,
Cooled down, nature developed.
Air and water plus points,
Up came the creatures!

A vintage man, an animal like;
Grew up savage, a Stone-Age man;
As the time passed by,
Grew up into modern man!

Nature mastered the man, survived;
Soon he learned to live and thrive,
Began swimming to rule the water,
Kept himself afloat!

Now began mastering the nature,
Took help of science to master others,
Began making mistakes, in excess;
Learnt to fly planes, ships afloat!

Developed industries and rockets,
Pollution resulted far and wide,
Disturbed nature with time!
As he learns to kill and thrive!

Develops the World,
Affected his life,
With countries to live and grow,
Moved into the space!

Left footprints where none ever been,
Explores universe, intergalactic way,
Fails to keep self control,
Scared to live on Earth!

The greed to control kept him flying,
Migrating to far planets,
Was all up in mind!
Leaving the Earth to decay.

Counter checks having failed,
Failed to unite the World,
Growth and destruction went all along,
Canniness grew amongst the nations!

Weapons of massacre he developed,
Tested them underground, in oceans;
Tested bombs, oil spills, affected marine life;
As devastation goes around!

Clock has almost turned full circle,
Nature is Climate, Climate is Nature;
Now turns violent affecting life,
Earth's devastation begins all over!

Flooding from rains, overflowing dams,
Forests on fire, unruly, wild;
Now troubled saving life all over,
Wars for hegemony sown around!

Bombing human habitations all over,
Unabated grew his greed,
Nomadic behavior on the rise,
Life's nothing but miserable!

Safe migration,
Locating new habitation up in mind,
To live on lifeless planets,
Only option left for now!

With "Blue diamond" in shambles!
Create an oasis in alien planet?
Planning to create life up there,
How could that be?

Starting life from Stone-Age there,
Faraway in a lifeless planet,
Is this possible! Would they succeed?
Imagination seems gone haywire!

Lucky or not only few could go?
Life won't be same, the rest would die!
Why not survive where we are?
Where we grew up so very fine?

Nature kept saving us,
Efforts for survival on the fence,
Science could destroy, betray mankind;
Now disaster is looming large!

Save the only "Blue Planet",
Where we live still thrive,
Forget landmass remote,
Help shelve the climate change!

Nature affected, climate changed;
Can we reverse it?
Forgone, can't mould to newer ways;
Forget to have nature in a planet beyond!

Slow it was for early man,
Nature developed climate good!
It's time, must concede to all,
Lost war to save, "My Nature, My World"!

Born with a Big-Bang,
Big-Crunch will take it away,
Till then wait for the celestial dance!
Near it is, not far away!

Call it a cosmic dance,
Dance of "Lord Shiva" we wait for,
In front of Nature,
Everyone is a slow learner!

4
My Nature, My World

My Nature, My World;
It was exclusively for all.
Who disturbed its glory?
Taking away its all!

I saw it giving all it had,
Distributing equally amongst all,
Livable since millions of years,
Sunshine, water, air for all!

Enough land it had, resources for all,
A landscape so beautiful, weather sublime!
An uneven surface, created a change,
Temperatures that suited all!

All was well for long,
Flora and fauna jelled together,
Giving space to all,
With air enough and food for all!

Who then created a hole amongst all?
Man, so intelligent developed it all.
Ambition took the toll, Oh dear!
Marked the land, disputes all over!

Calling it his own,
Restricted the entry,
Imaginary delineations,
Etched permanently in all!

Landscape changed once for all,
Swimming in rivers, floated on ships;
Crossing the borders without a pass,
Invites a full-scale war!

Gave torrid times to the marine animals,
Shaped cities for fun,
Felling the trees in forests,
Cared for none, forgot one and all!

Beasts in forests lived as they like,
Frolicking full of fun all their life;
Captured, restrained in locks and chains,
For one-upmanship, used them to his like!

With observation sublime,
Man, so talented, rebellious and mad;
Were the Scientists, took the World by storm;
Alas! Have sown the seeds of discord!

Scientists, the architects of science;
Unruly, a synergic they been;
Pillars of pollution, created machines,
Road to destruction thus created fast!

Handed over firearms, bombs and atom bombs;
Unleashed frequently, the decay grew fast;
The land which created scope,
Started kicking one and all!

My Nature, My World! Would it remain the same?
For it knows to teach them all,
"What thy sow, so shall thy reap",
A lesson it gave to all!

5
The Time Is Changing

Grew up,
To school,
Updating for the future,
Learnt to live and survive,
Let others grow and thrive.
Only thing changed,
Time slipped by!

Grew young,
Chased by time,
Envisioned with friends and teachers,
Prepared to work, live and survive;
Let others grow and thrive.
Only thing changed again,
Time slipped by!

Grew up,

Age catching up,

With time and experience, family and friends,

Lost few, gained new,

Only thing that changed again,

Time had slipped by!

6
Manipulating Nature

Himalayas rose high,
Up from lava, mud and stones;
On continental shift,
Rivers flowing deep in the valley,
Thin, narrow bed with flow so high!

Nature had it this way,
So created lasted time since formed,
What then tilted its balance off?
Thoughtlessness, insensitivity;
Enough to tilt it off!

For minor gains, imposed logic;
Despite warnings alongside,
Created dams so misplaced,
Right amongst Himalayas,
Now widespread over miles!

An ocean-like water body,
Inundated habitat all therein,
Destroyed habitation that existed,
Felling of trees, no effort to avert;
Fluctuating temperatures worsened it fast!

Moisture laden air, grew heavy,
Cloud formation perpetuating,
Acting as if coastally,
Spate of cloud now burst often!
Deadly results begin showing.

Rainfall lashes, landslides rising,
Rivers inundate, rips thru' its course;
Sub-Himalayan belt from East to West;
All affected thru' and thru'.
Deadly results its follow thru'.

Calamities are taking its toll,
Losses exceed, no one gain;
Dams are a liability, it's man-made;
Nature selectively weeds out the weak,
The loss is terrible all over.

Not much is lost, much to lose;
Its wake up time, reverse the trend,
For Himalayas are crumbling,
Will fall into, from where they arose!
Nature begins unleashing its power!

The misadventure goes off unchallenged,
Damages inflicted are very grave,
The force of devastation so intense,
Explosions tilt the balance to kill.
Implosions rock the Earth, breaks, collapse!

Nature is impassionate, relentlessly does it act;
Deterrence against, not ready to take;
Destroys creations so adverse,
As it resets upsetting flaw!
Manipulate the Nature! It manipulates all!

7
Break of Dawn

The night is nearly over,
Dawn about to break,
For it still is twilight,
Dawn a little away!

For many sleeps at this time,
As they miss the fun,
See transition happening,
Need to jump off bed!

It's happy time,
As the day dawns,
It's time to come out now and stray,
Walking early morn'!

With the night cover fading,
Shimmering stars begin to fade,
At the break of dawn!
As the Sun is rising far away,

As it draws to take control,
Welcome is the change!
Birds chirping and crows awake,
How they know, night's ticking away?

Music to ears is true for all;
Sound so nice to hear,
A breeze this time is so much fine,
Life begins afresh!

For the breeze so cool,
Air is fresh, so fresh to take;
A walk is fine,
Tunes up for the day!

So happy is the time for all,
Sun beginning to glow,
Orange glow awakens all,
For the lucky ones to see!

Imagining its glow is all we do,
For the mind to see,
Enjoying it, is just fun.
Over the horizon, far away!

Skyscrapers hide the sun,
Lightens up the sky,
Sky turns blue from grey,
For all to see the fun!

Difficult time now left behind,
Such is the daily norm,
So we see this every day,
Taking gloom away!

Everyone keeps waiting for,
As the day dawns;
The day next is today,
As it dawns today!

Wake up early every day,
At the break of dawn,
This happens time and again,
Everyone to see!

A breeze this time is so much fine,
See celestial dance!
A new day starts, thus;
At the break of dawn!

8
Floods All Over

Five life extinctions behind us,
Sixth extinction on!
History is rolling back again,
Thousands of species gone,
Many more waiting to go,
Climate change distinctly on,
Global warming threatening life,
Temperatures rising all over,
Melting glaciers afar,
Pollution is all over,
Engulfing the man!

Fossilized forests trapped in snow,
Releasing methane unrestrained;
Nature now is all violent,
Affects life of the man;
Rivers flooding with all its might,
Ocean rising fast,
Coastal cities to submerge!
"Matsya-Avatar" may save us all,

"Noah's-Ark" could be this time!
Millions await watery grave!

Torrential rains and cloud bursts,
Overflowing dams, flashing floods;
Threatens life all over!
City roads facing the brunt!
Air laden cars, man inflated;
Floaters, floating as a boat;
Ego that floats paralyses life,
Nature is in full control,
Things down to all time low;
Highways flooded, life submerged;
This is the "Road to Hell" we go;
With walls on either sides of roads,
Roads now turn waterways!
Nature in control!

Follies made were too many,
Leaves man on tenterhooks,
Nature altered, bites the man;
The intelligent stands ambushed,
Is this time he gets wiped off?
Like dinosaurs long ago!

Time so long has gone so fast,
In a spin, now introspect;
Occasion to go back in the past!
Accept mistakes, reverse the clock;
Reverse the clock, go back in time;
Dams created were big mistakes,
Water flow lacks control!
Why created with such controls?
Can you rule the nature this way?
Reassess, for what's been done;
Life is now on the edge of the sword!
Arms race, the factors;
Important are these, than ever more;
Fighting with gutsy men on borders,
Enemies all around, can't change borderline!
Expansionism issues, in neighborhood;
Disaster lurks, oblivious, can't ignore anymore!

History rolls back on extinction bid,
Would we perish, be lucky to survive!
Five life extinctions behind us!
Block the sixth, be our aim;
A miracle to be the hope! Then,
Pray for "Matsya Avatar" to save again,

As may "Noah's Ark" this time!
For nothing's now in your hand,
Survival on hope! For floods are on!
Need gills, teeth of sharks, hoping to survive!
With thoughts so bizarre!
Is mind running amuck?
Oh! Not really, not really!
For floods are on, floods are on!

9
Every Dark Cloud has a Silver Lining

It's end of June,
Humidity, heat at its peak,
As the easterly sets in,
It's time for monsoon to roll,
Cloudy days drawing in,
It's time to be back again!
The change so welcome to all of us,
The relief from the scorching heat,
As the wind draws the clouds,
Darker ones saw pushing in!

Overwhelms the sky from the east,
Seem closing in a hurry,
Moving with the wind,
Seem endlessly rushing in,
Sun behind the clouds, time and again;
Broad daylight fuses quickly.
It's getting dark with clouds,
Welcome is the change,
Happiness abounds all over!

The wind blowing keeps howling,
Bowing and swing the trees,
As nature sings a song!
Welcome is the change!
The roads turn grey to black,
Roads are wet darker they get,
As the drizzle turns sharp,
Clouds reflect on earth!
Nature looks now upside down!
A city life that never slows ever,
Is in standstill!

Dark clouds, thunders, roars;
Lightning flashes the sky;
As "Anvil Crawler" fills the sky!
As if hitting the ground!
Thunderous roar, all so soon;
Clouds seem not too high,
Different hues, in the clouds;
Flashes and roars up in the sky;
Coming from pretty deep!

Ah! It could be a loss out there,
Trees all washed up, looking so fresh;
As the nature stands renewed again!
It's bright green, shine around,
With puddles of water on ground!
The sky turns dark to grey,
Drizzle turning heavy!
Nature is flushed and clean!

Helter-skelter life appears,
Far and near, seek for shelters!
Earthy aroma all around,
Amazing nature, at its best!
So pleasing all around,
A perception varies!
Many gains, a few may lose,
Still a welcome sign!

Nature wet, very clear,
Pollution all but gone for now,
Sun goes in and out of clouds,
Glorious rainbow pops up,
It's perfect arc in the sky,
A divine "Indra-dhanush"!

Natural event, bestowed on us;
God's gift to us, in monsoons!
The breeze so cool, brightens lives;
"Every dark cloud has a silver lining"!
Benefits bestowed ends difficult times!

10
Nothing Stays the Same

When things go wrong!
Disconnected with everyone away,
Pandemic at its peak now,
Stay in peace, stay away.

Pray for the jinx to go away,
Despite those who take care,
Solace is hard to find,
Don't lose courage.

Bonds be stronger more than ever,
Let the beast melt away,
Sun is getting hotter here,
Somewhere snowing many feet!

It may blow hot and cold,
Erratic events come and go,
Pandemic will also be driven away!
For nothing ever stays the same!

11

World Times

Have we explored our World?
Exploration of Indian soil,
Is it all over?
What makes us explore the space?
More so of Mars,
Examine its soil?
Do we know our own?

Creating atmosphere where none exists,
Destroyed it in the World our own,
So eager to know of Mars!
Is it more habitable than our own?
Habitat and habitation on the rocks,
Affecting flora and fauna all over!

Rescue the Blue-Diamond for now,
Thinking of migrating!
Would it be so near?
Could we all go?
As we are at present!

How many may go?
Think of those left behind!

Would we be intelligent to know?
Who we are?
Where we came from?
The cost involved to go?
Would it be small or more?
The pollution done that proved costly.
Have we done enough for all?

With humanity, in poverty;
Destroying the World,
Searching new World!
Auto rejecting his own!
Creating dyssynergy all over!
Oh! What's gone wrong?
Dragon has sown the virus of flu,
To take control all over!

Spreading hatred, on a killing spree!
An unseen destroyer, small and wild;
Giving it a country name,
Indian, UK, Brazilian, African;

No glory, unjustified shame!
Call them Chao, Mao, Zhao,
If "Spanish flu" was one!
"Chinese flu" more than fine!

Now destruction all over,
Life itself is now on a toss,
There is complete chaos.
Were our priorities right!
With lots of wasted time!
With entertainment only in mind,
Nothing was set all right,
Now left with folded hands,
Asking help from all over!

Learn to be on our own?
Must be on our own!
Need to explore fault our own,
Needlessly exploring the space,
Must we pollute it all over!
Enough to clean the mess up here,
It's World Times, this is all for now!

12
The Midas Touch

It is a story of King Midas,
A Roman legend!
He earned a wish,
Alas! For his wish,
He got a curse,
Gold was the love.
The gold he wished for,
Have a golden touch!

So elusive was his wish,
He realized very soon.
As he quenched his thirst,
Water turned to gold.
Then his daughter, he touched;
Also turned to gold!
Life was a misery,
Realization complete!

Lesson did he learn,
Wishes so abusive,
The folklore gets infamous-
'Greedy Midas,
Turns you to gold',
No one would come near.
Crazy he became,
Illusive hopes,
Elusive were returns!

Realm of dream,
The wish he earned!
Greedy was he for sure,
Have everything,
Nothing to share,
Hoping all weird!
Illusive hopes,
Elusive you get!
Midas touch is but a curse!

Midas hopes,
Weird he gets!
The rejected ones,
In reality to live,

Desires that fulfills,
Must hurt no one,
Gold is not the lot,
Compassion one must seek!

13
The Man, the Keeper

The right arm of the team,
Is a team's man, works with a plan?
Accepts challenges, appraises the care,
Is a fact man, never a yes man!

Prepares to play it fair, is all that he always do,
The pitch he cares may not always be good.
Gives out his very best,
Doesn't care for his good!

Too many cuspids are at the feast,
Ready to have the heist!
Valued as the best judge of pitch,
Still ready receive the bricks!

While serving for the pitch,
Has never claimed his worth,
Despite giving off his best, remains unacclaimed;
Doesn't really care just speaks the truth!

A drummer of orchestra,
Has to shout it out!
When things are lost and forlorn,
Is a real utility man!

Even with good work,
He works on a toss.
Makes a solid comeback,
When there is chaos!

Keep things rolling!
While the team trails,
Going off track, get it back on rails;
The Keeper looks all fresh again!

Well versed with the facts,
Is the master of the riddles!
Spinners have made him mentally tough,
As the competitors struggle!

Expectedly works with straight bat,
Bows to examine the pitch!
Looks up behind,
To keep the figures right!

Used to carrying through the day,
From start till the end of the day,
Keeps an eye on the men,
Ensuring all is well with the pitch!

In the wink of an eye,
Knows fixing the evil,
Despite smart operators,
Stays one man wonder!

The arena created was great,
Many came rushing to have their problems fixed,
Some panted; some fainted,
Feel lucky that they are in!

The basket seems all full here, no more to take;
Season's ticket seems on sale,
With big-bucks on the rail,
Tough gets life in case if the team fails!

Despite all the efforts, despair is all he gets;
With all responsibilities on his head,
For the pitch undid all efforts,
Curator pays playing on deadly pitch!

Precious time gets wasted,
To manage infightings,
It isn't worth a penny,
In the process would lose many!

The pitch had lived a lifetime,
Worn out as it was,
Life, it's just over!
As it's he who calls it "The End"!

Are they even ready to see the bouncers hurled?
Facing them with all grace, as the fight is on;
Pitch is crumbling, difficult to read;
The team played together gave off their best!

Life is not all so easy in the middle,
The problem is of those managing the show,
Selected the team out of wits, least would they give;
Ready to get another team, is all do they care!

Would the day come ever, when they do it right?
For the pitch to be playable and is alright,
Keeper needs assistance to come from the likes,
Not in his control, the help comes from the unlike!

Being assisted by experienced to weather the storm,
Is aware, the best could fumble on the pitch!
At times, the team is tired, mind out of wits;
How would they perform expectedly as they should?

Wonder! Who the Keeper is?
Keeps plodding on,
Third umpires off arena,
Control the play, judge, sitting right there on!

The keeper is *Morton's man!
Sees off sufferings and pain,
Hush is all over, the pitch has been put to sleep;
Time is nearly over; it's but wake up time!

Morton's man, its Keeper, an Anesthesiologist as he is;
Works with perfection, learnt it playing safe;
Batsman handles softly; as he stands to care;
Musical setting on display as a drummer he works!

Accepts team as his own, a leader there to care;
Greets verbal straight right on when batters do a foul,
Calmly receive bouncers, all of them with grace;
Reflects expletives, now and then, right on their face!

Most important are the quivers, he regularly maintains;
As he returns the pitch, at the end of play;
Reputation keeps him going on, always plays for team;
Keeping the pitch ready, to let them play again!

---

* William T. G. Morton was an American Dentist and physician who publicly demonstrated the use of Ether for surgical anesthesia, annulled pain during surgery forever, at the Massachusetts General Hospital, Boston, USA, on 16 October 1846 celebrated as "World Anesthesia Day".

14
Power of Logic

How do you know?
How can you find?
When the truth trails!
Unfazed! Is all to do;
As falsehood prevail!
With no one there, to fight it right;
You are left to grind,
Knowing facts,
Not keen to find,
Isn't it a fact?
Run it down, as they may;
Fully aware of facts!
When one's right,
Just sit tight,
When the going gets tough!
A distant light that you can see,
Is the ray of hope!
Beacon of hope, all to you;
As the truth prevails,
An opportunity, to avail,

Struggler learns to fight!
This is how you do,
As the fight goes on,
Arguments excel!
Struggler prevails!

Pretensions must just fail,
Wait until,
Truth just shines!
May take some time,
Hard facts, judgment fair!
It is always delayed!
Power of logic!
Is all that work!
It's your time!
Truth finally prevails!
Such as is our amblem!
"Satyamev Jayate"!
Truth only triumphs!

15
Naturally Yours Play Me

Nature you are the only one,
So beautiful!
Need to be nurtured,
Survived time immemorial!
Need to keep it going,
For man to live and prosper,
Our greed!
Check imbalances.
To live or be outlived,
Enjoy the fruits of science,
Die because of it!
Be the cause of crash,
Over Atlantic or elsewhere!
Thunderous lightning!
The clouds be normal,
Kept low or high,
Above or below the plane flying!
Oh, Dear! You have been the cause!
Why fly so high?
Nature got tough,

Brought the ego down,
In a far away ocean!

Could we save our Earth?
Disappearing act of water,
Like on Mars.
Destroyed its nature!
Could it happen the same way?
On our Earth!
The water from Earth,
Goes into the Space
To another Earth, far away!
Save the nature.
Our greed!
Save Man!
Save the Earth!

16
Himalayan Tsunami

Tragedy unfolding,
Nature's fury, man-made;
Should worry us all!
Unexpected, unprepared;
So destructive was this,
Himalayan Tsunami was this!
This is tragedy!

It was a Tsunami, Man-made!
In Kullu!
Released water from the Dam!
On river Beas,
The river so blessed,
Became a curse!
It floods, where people stood;
Himalayan disaster was this!
Oh! My God!
Huge tragedy was this!

The spate washed away "The twenty-four",
The "twenty-four Engineers" of 'morrow!
Eighteen boys and six girls!
All washed away!
The dearest ones, from Hyderabad;
This was tragedy!

The most inept, ignorant at gates;
Clumsily, with no warning;
Acted recklessly!
Put on the gates,
Gush of water, off the gates;
Himalayan mistake it was,
This is tragedy!

Working on the dam,
Irrational, all along;
How many times, the gates got on?
Countless lives, lost for long;
No account, no accountability;
This is tragedy!

The flow unmarked,
Tsunami was that,
Washed away the future!

The future of families,
Loss so illogical,
Silently, it came;
And silenced them all!
Washed away years of efforts,
This is tragedy!

Preventable loss of lives was this,
Himalayan Tsunami was this,
Be logical to do the most trivial.
To avert this Himalayan disaster,
Work with passion,
Care for life,
See no more such tragedies!

17

Tolerance Eclipsed

Sun and Moon, often get eclipsed;
Though not for long,
Eyes fail to see,
Though, the heat's still on.
The warning is clear,
As the duo will come out,
Sooner than later,
Shining, smiling;
Brighter and clear!
Like in life,
To sustain,
Tolerance is a way of life!
For those destined to shine!
Eclipse is transient, surreal!

18
The Cry of the Day

It's the cry of the day,
The flora and fauna are the prey.
Man, you're responsible for this crime,
Cause of your ambition,
To lord the nature and make it all alone,
You forgot that the Mother Earth is for all.
Man, decrease your ambition,
Remember, the cry of the day,
Live to care for all!

Cause of your ambition.
Man, you invented, machine, engines and cars,
To lord the nature,
Bombs and atom bombs,
Before you get bombed off,
The earliest from the face of the earth,
Man, the most intelligent to have lived on earth,
Stop polluting the water, air and earth!
Decrease your ambition,
Remember, the cry of the day!
Live to care for all!

Cause of your Ambition,
To ease your lifestyle,
Man, you separated metals and minerals from the soil,
Surrounded now with heaps of mistakes;
Deforested, ecosystem deranged;
Afflicted its flora and fauna too!
Man must decrease your ambition!
Remember, the cry of the day;
Live to care for all!

To live long on Earth, Oh Man! You see;
Decrease your ambition!
Repair the ecology.
Clean the water, air and soil;
Breathable, livable, be the Earth, be it as before;
Let the fossilized man, not be remembered;
By the plastic he produced,
Footprints of pollution in space, depleted ozone layer;
Remember, the cry of the day,
Live to care for all!

19

Blocked and Choked

It is funny but real,
Comparisons surreal,
Arteries of city,
Traffic, noisy, pollution pollutes;
Blood flow to the heart,
Flushes, supplies and survive;
Often get blocked, choked;

Troubles and hurts!
Investigate, cure;
One, a man-made error,
Accessibility, accidents for sure;
Other, an error in man;
Check and let it flow,
Obstruction but kills!

20
Population over a Billion

Our population over a billion,
Is it our strength or weakness?
In fifty years grew three times,
Still multiplying against time,
Will make us number one, population wise!
Besides, decelerating the economic growth,
Economic disparity is on the rise,
With the poor becoming poorer!
Terrorism, fanaticism and robberies on the rise!

Population over a billion mark,
Is it our strength or weakness?
The need of the hour is to contain the growth,
Accept the norm of a child per family,
With the improved economic balance!
Shall we overcome the negative social trends!
Let child grow physically, economically, spiritually.
Strong family bond, a strong nation is born!

Think, a population over a billion mark,
Is it our strength or weakness?
Medical profession should check its role,
Itself a cause of population explosion,
Improved survival, failing birth control,
Increased female feticide, a new dimension of crime!
Altered the ratio with missing females,
Time to restore imbalances,
Contain growing population!

Imagine, with the population stabilization,
Shall India emerge as a regional power?
Then a Superpower!
Superpower not to flex the muscle power,
Help grow a strong, stable world!
Growing population would then become our strength,
Strength for stability, greed to vaporize!

21
Death a Life Anew

Death is inevitable,
An end of life,
When life becomes meaningless,
A phase of transition in process
When person forgets self,
Life processes worn out,
When nothing is left to do,
Shuts off from the world,
A sudden event follows,
Soul changes clothes.
Closing, shutting itself,
Enters a new World!
A process in its own,
Enters a new world of its own!

The same old nasty World!
Where it once been!
An old native,
Continues its narrative,
Renewing self!

Newer happenings begin,
Repeats similar life process!
Relearns to relive again,

Death acts as an angel!
Gets newer experience,
Shifting from older ones,
Gains new ones!
How useless possessions could get?
Your own flower, own jewel;
Finds a new owner!
Someone else take it away!
Where one goes,
No one ever knows!

To give the best to yourself,
Your once own ones,
Tread on learning's gained,
Un-forgetful of family ethos,
Live for times to come!
For then, the soul gets what you want.
Is it ever so simple?
Has it ever been!
Never has it, never will it be!

For it gets what it does!
It's the rule of nature!
"Whatever you sow, so shall you reap".
Could it be so good?
That you meet the lost ones,
Start life processes again!
Remember previous things,
Relive and undo past events!
Death does one thing,
It creates chances,
For self-correction,
Self-purification!
Till then, wait for the inevitable;
A new beginning!

22
Once in a Life Time

It was a day as normal,
Bright and sunny, as every day!
But, why it seems so bad today?
So ruffled the feathers seem today!
Why am I so distraught today?
Remember the years gone, way too back!
The same olden ways,
Those were the golden days!
The stories we heard,
Remember till the very day!

In the midst of busy days,
Living life careless ways,
Unprepared for times to come!
Times never remain the same all days,
"Buddha Purnima" was the day,
We lost a person the very next day!
A great person waited for the day,
A great soul left the World that day!
One who mattered foremost!
One who cared for all!

Expectations she had none,
Still used to be her best receiving all!
Mother's sister dear to us!
Welcomed all at home!
Gave new definition to her home!
Blessings always in the air for all!
Blessed was her soul!
Your mother as good as mine,
We all must care!

As time is passing,
These times,
No one knows,
When the time be over!
The day has come,
When the life's sinking!
Sun sets on her life today!
The life may be over next day!

Would be hard for one and all,
Life isn't the same today!
How can we forget?
The glee on your face!
Warmly you received,

Your laugh and love,
Used to share with all!

Will be remembered in times to come!
So shocking been the loss,
Benumbing news to one and all!
In these Covid times,
This is what we face!
Losing lives so precious to all,
Wish you were there,
You were there!
Still cherish your memories,
Long live in us and beyond!

www.ingramcontent.com/pod-product-compliance
Lightning Source LLC
LaVergne TN
LVHW061621070526
838199LV00078B/7373